The Shade

Kamiakin Middle School
14111 132nd Ave NE
Kirkland WA 98034

K.L. Denman

Orca currents

ORCA BOOK PUBLISHERS

Library and Archives Canada Cataloguing in Publication

Denman, K. L., 1957-

The shade / K.L. Denman.

(Orca currents)
ISBN 978-1-55143-933-4 (bound).--ISBN 978-1-55143-931-0 (pbk.)

I. Title. II. Series.
PS8607.E64S53 2008 jC813'.6 C2008-900400-0

Summary: As if her sister's wedding wasn't enough, now Safira has a
ghost to worry about.

First published in the United States, 2008
Library of Congress Control Number: 2008920733

Orca Book Publishers gratefully acknowledges the support for its publishing
programs provided by the following agencies: the Government of Canada
through the Book Publishing Industry Development Program and the
Canada Council for the Arts, and the Province of British Columbia
through the BC Arts Council and the Book Publishing Tax Credit.

Cover design by Teresa Bubela
Cover photography by Getty Images

Orca Book Publishers
PO Box 5626, Station B
Victoria, BC Canada
V8R 6S4

Orca Book Publishers
PO Box 468
Custer, WA USA
98240-0468

www.orcabook.com
Printed and bound in Canada.

11 10 09 08 • 4 3 2 1

For my sisters, Kendra and Tanya.
Remember Champ and the Ouija?

Acknowledgments

My gratitude to the generous spirits of the Great Aunties, Diane and Shelley. Very special thanks to Kimm Tarampi for the Filipino flavors, and to Nicole Foulkes for sharing a certain anecdote. The fine work of Melanie Jeffs, Orca Editor, is deeply appreciated too.

Life is a mystery, not a problem to be solved.

—Albert Einstein

chapter one

I'm wakened by a clanking rattle. It seems to be coming from the washstand. I squint across the dark room, past the other girls snoozing in their bunks. From my upper bunk I have a clear view, but I don't see anything unusual.

And then there's this tingling sense that someone is behind me. I turn slowly and meet the hollow stare of...who? I've never seen her before. She isn't one of the campers. She isn't a counsellor. She's wearing striped clothing, maybe blue and white. It's too dim to be certain. Her eyes are huge, but they're deeply set and reflect no glimmer of light. Or maybe the fall of jagged dark hair across her forehead shadows them? She looks so sad. So unbearably sad. She's standing near the foot of my bed, her face level with mine, and we gaze at each other. Neither of us speaks.

An instant later, my mind registers this certainty: She is not of this world. My throat constricts, strangling my scream. The choking sound I manage is no more than a whimper. I yank my sleeping bag over my head and hold it tight. Maybe I pant a little in the utter black of my cocoon. What is she doing? The sweat oozing from every pore on my rigid body itches. Has she come closer? I'm suffocating. Has she gone? I strain to hear something, anything, over the roar of my blood. I wait for a very long time.

When I can no longer bear the swelter of blind sweat and silence, the not knowing, I peek. Carefully. My fingers climb to the edge of the sleeping bag and inch it down past my eyes. I don't see her. I tug the cover down further and suck in a breath of cool air. I lift my head, turn it this way and that. Nothing. I stay like this, wide-eyed and tense, until the rising sun brings light and I can sit up. Everything is perfectly normal. I guess I doze a bit, because the next thing I'm aware of is the bell sounding to wake us. I watch the others get up, yawning and moaning. Who wears striped pyjamas? No one does.

I don't tell anyone at swim camp about her. I'm not exactly close to the other girls. Sure, I've had fun with them, but my dislike of the water has put a fence between us. They are so into it, so focused on improving their strokes. Me? Not.

Eight months ago, I begged my parents to send me to this camp. Swimming was my world. I used to dream about being a dolphin. But a lot can change in eight months. No, that's wrong. A lot can change in a moment. Especially if that moment was devastating. The sort of thing that yanks away your identity.

Back then, my parents came up with the money to pay for camp. When I changed my mind, it turned out they couldn't get a full refund. My dad really wanted me to go, no matter what. He seemed quite sure it would fix things. I couldn't get out of it.

For the first few days, the counsellors were determined to get me to participate. One of them sat with me and talked. "Come on, Safira. If you get in the water and just float, I'll be happy."

I said, "No, thanks. I'm working on my tan."

She asked if I was sick, did I need to talk to the nurse. She asked if there was a problem with the other kids. She asked if I was afraid. I answered no, every time.

I told her, "I just don't feel like it. I hate swimming. It's boring. The smell of chlorine is gross, and it wrecks my hair. I really wish I could have gone to a horse camp, but my parents sent me here."

"Hmm," she said. "I know people who ride horses. They say the best thing to do if you fall off is get right back on. Conquer your fear."

"I'm not afraid, okay? And isn't summer camp supposed to be fun?" I smiled at her. "Don't worry about me. I'm totally fine just watching and reading a book."

She finally backed off. I guess since I participated in all the other activities, she figured I was all right. Maybe she thought I was a brat, but at least she left me alone.

Anyway. Today is the last day, and everyone is racing around, trying to find their stuff. There's a lot of fake gagging as filthy clothes are dropped into suitcases. By the time my things are packed, the sad girl seems hazy crazy. Nothing more than a bad dream.

When my parents arrive to pick me up, I see an eager light in Dad's eyes. He's smiling so hard his face looks deformed. He hugs me and says, "So? So, how did it go?"

"Good," I say.

"Oh, that's wonderful, honey. Great news! What was your time for the backstroke? Better?"

I don't want to take that light out of his eyes. That light is hope. He's hoping everything is back to the way it was.

Mom cuts in and says, "Do I get a moment here?" She steps close and hugs me. "I missed you, Safira."

Dad keeps grinning. "Yeah, me too. You look good, kid. Let's get your bags into the car and then you can tell us all about it on the drive home."

"Dad, there's nothing to tell. I didn't swim. I had fun doing lots of other stuff. Campfires, games, crafts. But I told you I wouldn't swim. And I didn't."

The light disappears. He looks away. "Oh," he says. And that's it. Oh.

We don't drive home in silence. Mom comes up with nonstop chatter about The Wedding. My sister, Mya, is getting married soon, and it sounds like things are intense. Mom's voice keeps rising as she runs through the list of preparations. "The cake has been ordered. Mya finally decided on blue for the church decorations. The hair appointments are booked. I've had no luck finding shoes to go with my dress."

On and on she goes. Ribbons, music, flowers, menus...I really don't want to hear it, but it's better than the dead quiet surrounding my father.

Ten minutes after I'm home, I call my best friend. "Hey, Trinity."

"Safira!" she screeches. "You're back! Can you come over? Now?"

"For sure," I say. "At least I think so. I'll ask."

"Tell your mom I have a crisis and I need you."

I have to smile. Trinity is always having a crisis. "Okay, I'll be right there. I've got something to tell you too."

"Yeah? Is it about swimming?"

"As if. I'll tell you when I get there, okay?"

Mom starts to give me guilt about taking off so soon, but Mya saves me. She doesn't do the saving on purpose. It's more like an accidental rescue. We hear her before we see her. She slams through the back door, yelling, "I can't believe we're getting fruitcake! I've realized that fruitcake is just wrong!"

She's clearly having one of her "Mya Mia Moments." She bursts into the kitchen and notices my presence. Sort of. She says, "Hey, Safira. You're back. Was camp fun?"

She doesn't wait for me to answer. She never does. She looks at Mom and says, "So like I was saying, I don't want fruitcake. No way. I want carrot cake."

Dad rolls his eyes. Mom frowns and starts defending fruitcake.

I go to Trinity's.

chapter two

Trinity drags me into her room the moment I arrive and closes the door. "Let me look at you," she says. "Hmmm. Yep. You've changed in the past two weeks."

I raise an eyebrow. "It's probably just my tan." I do have an excellent tan.

"Nope," Trinity says, "it's not your tan. It's something else." She tilts her head to one side and taps her cheek with a dainty finger as she studies me. Trinity is a tiny person, though not as short as her Filipino mother.

Her personality is not tiny. She reminds me of a hummingbird, a bright lively creature but hardly delicate. She vibrates with energy. That sound hummingbirds make, like the light sabres in *Star Wars* movies, reminds me of Trinity too. She whirs with ideas, sometimes talking so fast everything blurs together.

"Darn it," she says. "I can't put my finger on it. What happened to you, Safira?"

I shake my head. "You first. What's the crisis?"

Trinity's eyes widen. Her voice drops to a whisper. "I got into trouble. Really freaky trouble."

"With who?"

"Not who," she says. "What."

"What?"

"Right. What." Trinity grabs a book from her nightstand and hands it to me. "Look at this."

The book's cover is plain black, no title, no picture. "What is it?" With Trinity, it could be anything.

"I picked it up in the secondhand book-store. It's sort of occultish."

"Occultish? As in magic or something?" No surprise there. Trinity loves that stuff.

"Not exactly. It tells you how to leave your body."

A shiver snakes through me. I hand the book back. "Are you kidding me?"

"No." She shakes her head. "Trust me, it's for real. I know because I did it."

"You *what*?"

"I did it. And it was terrible, Safira. I went through all the steps, meditating with a candle and stuff, and then... whoosh! There I was, floating around on the ceiling, looking down at myself sitting there."

"No way!"

"Way! But the worst part was that I wanted to get back into my body and I couldn't. I felt like I was going to drift into space or something. I was so scared, you wouldn't believe it."

"Uh, yeah, I believe it. That was a crazy thing to do. So what happened? How did you get back?"

She shrugs. "I don't know. One minute

I was panicking, totally desperate, and the next, I was just back. Snap. Thank God."

"Wow. Trinity, I don't think you should do that again."

"Too right I'm not doing it again." She shudders. "I'm going to stick to Tarot cards and spells. And ESP."

I stifle the impulse to roll my eyes. This is one of the things I do and don't like about Trinity. It's fun sometimes to hear her nutty ideas, but other times, I just wish she'd get over it. I am so *not* into that stuff. Except, well, there is that little episode from camp, and I do want Trinity's take on it.

"So what about you?" she asks. "I know something happened. Did you swim?"

I give her a look. "What do you think?"

She sighs. "Sorry. I just thought the camp might have...inspired you."

"It didn't."

"Okay," Trinity says. "So tell me."

"Right." I take a deep breath and I tell her about the striped girl. Trinity listens straight through, her dark eyes widening and narrowing. She makes little gasping sounds here and there.

When I'm done, she wraps her arms around herself and says, "Too cool."

"What? Cool? It wasn't cool, Trinity. It was freakin' scary."

"Yeah, of course. But it's still cool." She gets this wistful look on her face. "I sure wish I could see a ghost."

"Trinity?"

"Yeah?"

"Trust me," I say, "you don't want to see a ghost. If it even *was* a ghost."

"Oh," she says, "it was a ghost all right."

"How do you know?" I ask.

"Because it was classic. See, the thing is, Safira, you handled it all wrong. If *I* had been there, I would have asked her what she wanted."

I raise an eyebrow. "Excuse me? Ask her what she wanted?"

Trinity nods. "Yes. I've researched ghosts. And when they're hanging around like that, it's because they have unfinished business."

"Unfinished business?" I ask. "She didn't have any business with me. I don't even know who she was."

"I didn't say you did. But since you were able to see her manifest, you should have helped her. Find out what she had to say. Maybe she was murdered or something and she wants the murderer caught."

"Jeez," I moan. "Trinity. I was scared, okay? I thought she was going to murder *me*."

Trinity waves a hand. "Don't be silly. How could she do that? Ghosts don't have any substance."

"No? Then how did she make the clanking noise?"

It takes Trinity a minute to answer that one. "Hmm. You don't know for sure *she* made the sound, but if she did, maybe it was through telekinesis?"

"Yeah," I say sarcastically. "Maybe. Look, the other big problem I have with this whole thing is, I don't even believe in life after death."

Trinity gives me a pitying look. "I know," she says. "Maybe that's why you saw her? So you could believe."

I sigh. "Don't you have any other explanation? I mean, even though it didn't feel like a dream, that's probably all it was. We were telling ghost stories at camp—I bet I just imagined it."

More pity from Trinity. "Yeah. And on Tuesdays I'm a tall troll. C'mon, Safira. You wouldn't be so freaked if it was a dream. It happened."

chapter three

"You bought *another* dress?" Mom's face has paled to white. Only her nose is bright pink and quivering. This is a face a smart person would run from. Lucky for me she's looking at Mya.

"Mom, please, just chill." Mya rolls her eyes and sighs. "It's no big deal. How am I supposed to know what I'll feel like wearing that day? It's the biggest day of my life. I can't predict my mood ahead of time."

"*Two* wedding dresses?" Mom actually spits when she says "two."

"I don't get your problem. I can return the one I don't wear. It makes perfect sense. One of the dresses is extremely elegant, all smooth and sleek, right? The other one is lacy, with satin and a touch of pink—it's the romantic look." Mya ponders. "Really, I wouldn't mind having a third one, maybe that one with the sheer sleeves, in case it's a bit chilly..."

Mom cuts her off. "A third one? Unbelievable. Mya, are you telling me these dresses fit you perfectly, right off the rack? They don't require any alterations? And you don't feel the slightest degree of guilt for taking advantage of the bridal shop like this?"

"Oh." Mya waves a hand. "I went to a different shop for the second one. And one of the dresses does fit a bit bigger than the other. But see, that's another factor to consider. What if I gain or lose a few pounds before the wedding? If I only have one dress, it might not fit." Her voice rises. "And then what will I do?"

"Gee," Mom says, "I don't know. Why don't you order doubles of everything? Two bouquets, two limos. Then of course the groom will need two tuxedos, and I'm certain there ought to be at least two reception halls to choose from..."

"Mom." Mya squeezes her eyes shut. "Please. I can't take this stress."

"The problem with you, young lady, is you aren't ready for this. You're only twenty years old. You don't even know who you are. And you're getting married? What a joke!" Mom's hand flies up and covers her mouth. It's like she can't believe she said that. And then her hand falls down and she shrugs. She's not taking it back.

Tears well in Mya's blue eyes, but for once, she doesn't start yelling. Quietly, she says, "Look who's talking. At least I'm not pregnant. And I know who I am all right. I'm the person who can't wait to get out of this joke of a family."

She glares at Mom who glares right back, and I say, "I'm going over to Trinity's."

I don't even know if Mom heard me. There are tears in her eyes now too.

Trinity is happy to see me. "Do you want to go to the beach?" she asks.

"The beach?" I shake my head. "As in, swimming?"

"Okay." She sighs. "Forget I mentioned it. We've got something important to work on anyway. I've been doing some ghost research and I'm wondering—were there any antiques in your cabin?"

I say, "Huh?"

"You know, old furniture. Like old dressers or mirrors or paintings."

"All that stuff looked old to me." I shrug. "Why do you want to know?"

Trinity frowns. "*All* of it was old? Hmm. See, sometimes the spirit of a person gets attached to a piece of furniture."

I raise my eyebrows. "Really?"

"Yes, really. It could be something the person owned. They stick close to it because it's familiar. Or," she adds, "the item in question had something to do with their death."

"Oh, right." I giggle. "Like a painting fell on their head and killed them?"

Trinity puts her hands on her hips. "It's not funny, Safira! If you would just concentrate for one minute and try to remember any unusual items, we might be able to figure this out."

"Figure what out?" I ask.

She stamps a foot. "Who your ghost is, of course!"

I'm surrounded by crazy people. Everywhere I go, there they are. Trinity is waiting for me to say something. I tell her, "Now that I think about it, the washstand looked totally ancient."

Her eyes light up. "Omigod! That makes perfect sense. She came out of the washstand."

I blink. "Yes, of course. That must be it. She lives in the washstand." Sometimes, it's just easier to go with the flow.

"Excellent." Trinity flits over to her desk and grabs a pen and paper. "Now, describe it."

"Describe what?"

"The washstand, you idiot. What did it look like?"

"Now I'm an idiot?" I ask.

Trinity waves her pen. "Sorry. But please, just try to get into this, will you?"

"Fine. Whatever. It was shaped sort of like a block. It was probably painted white at one time, but it's all dinged up and yellowish now. It has an old sink set in the top and...Jeez, I don't know. It could be in one of the pictures I took. Why don't I check that out?"

Trinity's eyes go round. "For sure," she breathes. "There might even be an aura around it."

"An aura around the washstand?" I can't keep the sarcasm out of my voice.

Trinity's mom chooses that moment to call from the kitchen, "Triniteee! I've made *lumpia*."

"Coming, Mamang," Trinity calls back. She looks at me. "Do you want some *lumpia*?"

When Trinity first asked me that question, about five years ago when we started hanging out, I said no thanks. I mean, *lumpia*? It sounded disgusting. But it turned out Trinity's mom makes fabulous Filipino food, and *lumpia* are yummy deep-fried spring rolls.

"Are you kidding?" I ask.

Her eyes narrow. "Then you're going to show me the picture of the washstand?"

"What is this, blackmail for *lumpia*?"

She tosses down her pen and stands up. "You got it."

I follow Trinity to the kitchen where Mrs. Turner greets me with a hug around my waist. "Ah, Sapira!" Mrs. Turner does not do the letter *F*. "I'm glad you're here. Now hurry up, sit down."

She shoos me to the table, and I grab a chair next to Trinity's five-year-old brother, Kipp. "Hey, cupcake," I say.

He sticks out his tongue and says, "You better watch it. I know Kung Fu."

"No way," I say.

"Wanna bet?" he asks. "I'll show you." He leaps from his chair and strikes a pose. Then his arms fly about like he's fighting off a mad bee attack and he starts throwing out kicks. All the while he yells stuff like, "Hu! Ha! Ga!"

Mrs. Turner watches the performance in silence for about ten seconds. Then she calmly picks him up by the back of his pants and sets him down in his chair. "We do not Kung Pu in the kitchen," she tells him.

Trinity snorts. "No poo of any kind, I hope."

Kipp makes a face at her and then grins fiercely at me. "See?"

"Amazing," I say. I take a bite of *lumpia* and glance at Trinity. She's smiling at her little brother and the smile says it all: she loves him to bits. My sister has never looked at me that way. Never. The lump in my throat has nothing to do with the food.

chapter four

When Trinity finds out I have my camp pictures on film that hasn't been developed, she starts moaning. "Film? Why didn't your mom let you take her digital camera?"

"I don't think she trusted me with it. Didn't want to take any chances on it getting broken before the wedding, right? That would be the end of the world."

Trinity snorts. "That bad, eh?"

"Oh, yeah. She also wanted me to test one of those disposable cameras. Mya plans to hand them out to guests at the wedding and have them take candid shots."

"Well then," Trinity says. "How about we get the camera and take it to that one-hour photo place at the drugstore?"

"I guess. I'll have to ask my mom for some money too."

"All right then." Trinity waves a hand. "Let's go."

On the way to my house Trinity starts talking about auras and how she's been trying to see them. "It would be so cool. You can tell how someone is feeling, just by reading their aura."

"Is that right?" I ask.

"Yeah. The book I read says everyone sees auras when they're little. Then for some reason, we grow out of it."

"Uh-huh," I say.

"I think it's true." She gives me a sideways look. "Growing up makes us sort of...dull."

"No way. I can't wait to grow up. Look at Mya. She gets to do whatever she wants."

We've reached my front door and stop there. Trinity says, "Yeah. But is she happy?"

I shrug. "How would I know?"

Trinity narrows her eyes. "You don't know if your sister is happy?"

"Aren't people supposed to be happy when they're getting married?"

Trinity sighs. "I guess. But you should be able to tell."

"Oh, come on," I say. "You know what she's like. She barely notices I'm alive. She hardly ever says two words to me. She's way older than me, right?"

"True." Trinity studies me closely. "But she's still your sister. And she's around."

I shake my head. "She's not around me. She's always been this super-smart, busy person. Always knows what she wants and goes for it. She doesn't have time for me. And when she got engaged last year, I knew that was it for us. We'll never be close."

Trinity pats my arm. "You're like a sister to me, Safira."

I grin and give her a hug. "Thanks. You too. Come on, let's get the film, and I'll see if Mom's around to give me some cash."

We didn't notice the car pulling up to the curb on the street, but the male voice that mocks us is hard to miss. "Aw, isn't that cute. Don't stop on my account, girls."

It's Lino, Mya's jerk of a fiancé. We turn and stare at him. He swaggers up the driveway, his eyes hidden behind a pair of dark shades. His mouth is set in the sneer that is his version of a smile. And he's wearing his uniform—low-riding black jeans and a white T-shirt.

"What?" he says. "No hug for your new big bro, Safira?" He looks at Trinity. "And you can give some love too, little chickie."

Trinity wrinkles her nose. "I don't think so. Little chickie? Are you for real?"

Lino's sneer is gone, replaced by a blank mask. "Oh, yeah," he says softly. "I'm real all right. Now if you kids don't mind, I'm here to get my *woman*." He shoves past us and opens the door. "Mya?" he yells. "Come on, move it. We got things to do."

And Mya's there in a flash, wrapping her arms around Lino, saying, "Hey, Hon, I'm here. Right where you want me."

"I'd rather you were waiting outside, like your snotty little sister," he growls. He takes hold of Mya's long ponytail and gives it a tug.

Mya startles and says, "Hey!"

Before she can say anything else, he plasters an arm around her. It's an arm that says he's taking what's his. "Come on, Babe," he says. "I'm just playing around. Don't be so touchy." Then he propels her toward his car.

Mya glances back at us, eyes narrowed, one side of her mouth pulled up into something that isn't a smile. I can't read her expression. It's like she's embarrassed, yet she's daring us to notice.

I blurt, "Bye, Mya."

Her smile is real this time. She gives a tiny wave. Then they climb into the car and with the usual squeal of tires, they're gone.

"What a creep." Trinity says.

"Yeah," I agree. And even though it's a warm afternoon, I shiver. "Blech," I add.

"What does she see in him, anyway?"

"You've got me." I walk through the open

door and head upstairs to my room. "I'll just grab the film, Trin. Be right back."

The truth is, I need a minute alone. Maybe it's the way I've been raised, in a family that keeps quiet about feelings. Right now my feelings are messed up, and I need a quick review. What happened in the past few minutes? We talked about growing up. I thought about losing Mya. Trinity made me feel better. We were trashed by Lino. There was that thing he did to Mya's hair. What else? The shiver. What *is* that? I've been getting shivers off and on ever since that time in the pool...

"Safira? Is that you?" There's Mom, actually aware of my existence for a change. Okay, so she always was, up until the weird wedding world took hold.

"Yeah, just a minute." I pick up the film, go back downstairs and find Trinity hovering by the front door. "Hey," I say, "come in."

She gives me a faint smile and follows me into the kitchen. Mom is sitting at the table, frowning, as she sorts through a stack of paper. It takes a minute before she looks up. "There you are. And you too, Trinity. How are you?"

"I'm good," Trinity answers. "How are you, Mrs. Nelson?"

Mom shakes her head. "I'm muddled. I'd forgotten how much work a wedding can be. Not that I ever really knew. Mine wasn't exactly a big splash..." Her voice trails away.

Mom doesn't tell the whole story now, but I've heard it many times. Mya had her first "Mia Moment" before Mom and Dad got married. Mom was only twenty, and their wedding was a small celebration. Just family and a few close friends. She says it meant a lot to their parents. She often sighs when she adds that she doesn't regret it, she'd do it again because her and Dad are still in love. There's always the final sigh when she tells us they were very young.

"At least it'll be over soon," Trinity says. "Weekend after next?"

"Oh my Lord," Mom replies, "don't say it like that. Is it so soon? It is, isn't it?"

"Yes, Mom," I say, "it really is. So I should get my camp film developed and make sure it worked, right?"

"Camp film?" You can actually see her mind shifting gears. "Oh, yes, it would be great to see your pictures." She pauses. "Let me see if I have some money."

She digs into her purse, and her brow wrinkles. "Maybe I'll have to go with you so I can put it on my credit card. Ah! Here's a ten. Will that be enough?"

"I don't know," I say. I hate this. It seems like my parents have been broke ever since Mya got engaged.

Mom scrounges in her purse again and pulls out a five. "There. This ought to do it."

chapter five

Once we're outside and on our way, I mutter, "Wow. It sure seems like weddings cost a lot."

"I guess." Trinity shrugs. "But if I ever get married, it won't be a big waste."

"As in, you won't marry a loser?" I ask.

"No. Well, yes, that too. But I meant I'd have a green wedding. It's way cooler. I'd get a previously loved gown. *Everything* would be secondhand. Okay, not the food, of course. And if we got diamonds, I'd make sure they weren't mined by slaves."

Her face goes dreamy. "I'd get married in a woodland garden. Everyone would wear costumes. They'd dress up as fairies or birds or elves. And I'd ask them for gifts like donkeys and goats to be sent to third world families."

"Right," I scoff. "How do you send a donkey halfway around the world?"

Trinity rolls her eyes. "You don't send the actual donkey. You send money to a charity and *they* buy the donkey."

"Oh." I think about this for a minute. "I'd really like to give Mya and Lino an actual donkey."

Trinity bursts out laughing. "That would be hilarious! Do it."

"How about a chicken?"

"Yeah, a chicken too." Trinity starts clucking and I join in.

It's really bad timing for clucking, because we've reached the mall parking lot and suddenly there are people everywhere—including a group of the ultra-popular girls.

They look at us with disgust and one of them says, "Wow. You are sooo immature."

I feel my face go red, but Trinity giggles and says, "Lighten up, Nat. Haven't you heard? This is the latest in voice training. It builds vocal range."

Now Nat's face turns red. Everyone knows she's a wannabe famous singer. "You are so full of it, Trinity."

Trinity looks dead serious. I don't know how she does it. "Fine. Don't believe me then. But if I were you, I'd at least check it out." And she flits past them without a second glance.

I follow, hoping my fake show of cool is good enough. I hate getting caught acting like a kid. It's fine when it's just me and Trin, but around those girls...I don't know. Sometimes, I want to *be* those girls.

Once we're safely inside Trinity emits a final cluck, and I'm giggling again. I ask, "Do you think she'll try to find lessons on clucking for voice?"

"Maybe," she says. "For all I know, it's true. Makes sense, don't you think?"

"Absolutely," I say.

We turn in the roll of film and then spend an hour checking out makeup and jewellery. There's a really cute pair of earrings I'd like to get, but there's only enough money left over for a bag of chips. Hopefully, Mom didn't want the change back.

And then we pick up the pictures. Trinity insists we open the envelope as soon as we leave the store. When she finds one with the washstand in the background, she actually stops breathing.

"Look at it!" she gasps. "Omigod! Look!"

chapter six

I'm afraid to look at the picture. There will be a ghoul face in the mirror above the washstand. Or a grinning skeleton with its bony finger pointing. Or the sad girl will be standing next to the camp girls, crying.

None of these things are in the picture. There are my pals, showing off their crazy hairstyles, and the washstand behind them. And that's it.

"What?" I ask Trinity. "It was just a hair contest the counsellors put on when it rained one day. Trust me, those girls don't always look like freaks."

"I'm not worried about their hair, Safira. Look at the light behind them. See? It's an aura."

I squint at the picture. There *is* a rather strange glow around the washstand. I don't remember noticing it when I was at camp. And then it clicks. "There's a light bulb above the stand. That's all it is."

"You think?" She asks. "Then why is the light brightest down low, instead of over their heads?"

"Then it's the flash from my camera, reflected in the mirror. Come on, Trin, there's a simple explanation for this."

Trinity shakes her head. "I wouldn't be so sure about that. This light doesn't look right. It looks sort of greenish."

"It does?" Again, I examine the picture. She's right; there is a tinge of green in the light. Still. "Look, you can see a bit of the wall there, by the mirror. It's sort of green. That would explain it."

Trinity squints at the strip of wall behind

the girls and then plants her hands on her hips. "That is not green. That's more like vomit yellow. Why are you so determined to ignore the evidence?"

Before I can answer, she goes on. "I'll tell you why. You had an experience you can't explain. Since you can't explain it, you want to pretend it didn't happen. It's like what happened to you in the pool. You're not being logical, Safira."

"Oh, really?" I say. "Maybe *you're* the one who's not logical. The pool thing has *nothing* to do with this. And if you showed this picture to anyone who didn't know about the...whatever she was, they wouldn't notice anything funny."

"See?" Trinity says. "You're in denial. You can't even admit you saw a ghost. Hmm. I wonder. You *are* under a fair bit of stress. Tell me, do things around your house go missing? Or do objects go flying around?"

We've reached a bus stop with a bench, and I sit down. I glare at her. "What?"

Trinity sits beside me. "You can tell me the truth. You know you can."

I sigh. "No, Trinity. Objects do not go missing or fly around."

"Good. I had to ask because it occurred to me that you could be dealing with a poltergeist. They cause those sorts of things."

"Jeez, Trinity. Why can't you leave this alone?"

"Why can't you see that you need to do something?" Trinity is practically vibrating. "It's like this. If this girl has been murdered or whatever, and she's come to you for help, how can you turn your back on her?"

I jump to my feet. "Because I don't know what to do about it, that's how. She shouldn't have asked me, okay? Besides, she didn't ask me anything. She just stood there."

"So?" Trinity says. "You can't expect her to talk. I have an idea for that, though. We'll try to contact her with the Ouija Board. And we'll contact the camp and ask them if they know the history of the washstand."

Right. She is so darn loopy, if she wasn't like the sister I wish I had, I'd ditch her so fast... "Whatever. Fine. Can we go home now?"

"Do you want to sleep over tonight so we can try the Ouija?" she asks.

I get that shiver again. "I don't know. I'll have to ask."

Trinity grins. "All right! This is going to be so cool."

I decide I won't ask and tell her my parents said no. Maybe I should start clucking again, because the truth is, I'm scared of Ouija boards. It's not that I believe in them or anything, but why take a chance on something like that?

It turns out that my house is even scarier than the Ouija. When I get home, Mom and Mya are at it again in the kitchen. I take refuge in the living room with Dad.

"How are you doing, Safira?" he asks. But he looks tired, not really interested.

I tell him I'm fine and switch on the TV.

I guess I misjudged him. He switches the TV off and looks at me closely. "No, really. How are you?"

"Really," I say, "I'm fine."

"Good. That's good. And, uh, what about the swim team? Any chance you've changed your mind?"

"No chance," I say.

"Aw, Safira. Are you sure? I know last year was tough for you, but..."

"No, Dad. It's history."

"But..." He doesn't get any further. The volume of the fight in the kitchen just went up about ten decibels.

Mom yells, "First you don't want any children at your wedding. No children, for heaven's sake. A wedding is not a stage production. It's a community celebration, the community of your near and dear ones. Your cousin is so hurt that she can't bring her baby. Worse, you didn't even ask your sister to be a bridesmaid!"

I bite hard on my lower lip and keep listening.

"Mom. You know why I couldn't ask Safira. She would be a junior bridesmaid, and Lino didn't have anyone to be a junior groomsman. End of story."

"Oh, I'm sure you could have found someone, if you'd bothered to try. And now. Now you're saying your best friend is a loser and you don't want her for a bridesmaid either? Think about that, Mya."

Mya screeches back, "Jill doesn't care about me anymore, Mom! She's hardly helping at all. And every time I try to talk to her about the wedding, she changes the subject."

I mutter, "Maybe she's sick to death of it."

Dad gives me a look.

Mya continues. "I asked her to go with me and Lino to check on the guys' suits and she said no. She didn't even have a reason. So when I bugged her some more, she almost started crying and finally said she can't stand Lino. Can you believe that? How can she be my best friend and hate my man?"

"She's not the only one," I say. I catch Dad's eye and see his look is keener now. Thoughtful.

We listen on and hear Mom saying, "Jill's entitled to her opinion, Mya. Just because she doesn't like Lino doesn't mean she doesn't care about you. Please, think about this. Are you really willing to cut her out of your life? She's been a good friend to you for years."

"Some friend," Mya hisses.

Mom's voice softens, but I can still hear her. "Why don't you and Jill go out for coffee? Just the two of you. Try to work it out."

"Lino doesn't want me to see her. I told him what she said and he said to forget her. He said no real friend would hurt my feelings like that."

"Oh," says Mom, "I don't know. Real friends are sometimes the only ones who can tell it like it is. She's never let you down before."

I tune them out and ask Dad, "Would it be okay if I slept over at Trinity's?"

He doesn't answer right away. When he finally does, he says, "So you don't like Lino either?"

I shake my head. And then the *way* he asked this question strikes me as interesting.

Is he saying he dislikes Lino? I don't usually ask my parents about their feelings, but this seems like a breakthrough moment. "Dad, how do *you* feel about Lino?"

His mouth presses into a hard line, and I see a tiny muscle twitching in his jaw. But he only says, "Seems like your sister loves him and she's made up her mind. We can accept that or make her a stranger."

"What do you mean?" I ask.

He sighs. "If we refused to go along with this, she might shut us out of her life."

I don't think this would be anything new, at least for me. But before I can ask another question, he adds, "Parents and children don't always agree on what's best. You should understand that, Safira. You know how I feel about your swimming, and yet—"

I cut him off. "Dad. Stop."

His gaze is full of sorrow. "You're such a natural. I know you had that incident, but if you kept trying, you'd get over it."

I turn away from him and mutter, "I don't want to try."

"But, honey..."

"Can we just forget about this? And can I sleep over at Trinity's?"

He rubs his eyes and says, "Fine with me. Go ahead."

chapter seven

The only light in Trinity's room comes from the flickering candles. The major smell in the room comes from the incense. "It's all about creating the right atmosphere," she says.

We sit cross-legged on the floor with the Ouija board between us. We poise our fingers on the pointer dealie. Nothing happens. We wait. Nothing happens.

"Trinity?" I whisper.

"Shhh!" she whispers back. "Keep

concentrating. Hold the image of the girl in your mind."

My legs are starting to cramp, and I'm trying very hard to *not* think about the girl.

"Picture her hair," Trinity says, "her eyes. Her stripes. Bring all the details back into your mind, Safira."

As she says this stuff, I do see the girl again. My scalp tingles. The hair on the back of my neck quivers. The incense tickles my nose. I sneeze, and the pointer goes flying.

"Jeez, Safira," Trinity grumbles. "Now we'll have to start over."

"Maybe we should take a little break," I say.

"No. We were getting somewhere. I could feel it. Come on, Safira, it's important."

"Fine," I mutter.

"I think we should try asking a question," Trinity says. "Let's see. I know!" She closes her eyes, and in a low voice she asks, "Is the spirit of the girl we seek present?"

The pointer starts to move. Slowly.

"Are you pushing it?" I hiss. "Stop pushing it!"

"I'm not doing anything. Look, I'm barely touching it."

It's true. Her fingers are hardly contacting the pointer. My fingers are almost off it too. The pointer picks up speed and slides directly to the word *YES*.

"Omigod," I breathe.

"She's here." Trinity breathes.

"Now what?" I ask.

Again, Trinity closes her eyes and deepens her voice. "Do you need help?"

The pointer remains in place.

"That must mean yes," Trinity whispers. She's vibrating with excitement as she asks, "Who are you?"

For a second, nothing happens. And then the pointer starts sliding again. It goes to the letter *S*. It pauses, then moves to *I*. Then back to *S*. It takes a short trip to *T*, zips over to *E*, slides to *R*, then back to *S*. And that's it. It has spelled out the word *SISTERS*.

"Wow!" Trinity says. "I've tried this so many times and it never worked."

"It never worked?" I ask.

"Nope. You see how important this must be? And now we know she was likely murdered by her sister!"

I blink at her. "How do we know that? You just asked her who she is, and it spelled sisters. Which, if you ask me, doesn't tell us anything."

"Safira, the Ouija never gives a straight answer. We have to interpret."

"What if we can't?" I ask.

"Please, just be patient. And quiet. You're spoiling the atmosphere. We need to ask more questions." Again with the closed eyes. "Did your sister kill you?"

Nothing happens.

Trinity sighs. "Okay. Wrong question. Let's see. Where did you live?"

Nothing.

"Do you want us to help you?" she asks.

The slider gives a slight jerk and then shuffles to *YES*.

I am totally creeped out. But I ask the next question. "How?" I croak.

The slider trembles, as if it's going to go somewhere, then stops.

"What should we do?" Trinity asks.

Again, nothing.

She tries more questions, but it's obvious the Ouija is done.

chapter eight

I never should have gone along with the Ouija idea. I'm having a crisis. I can't explain the appearance of the girl or the actions of a cheap plastic thing sliding around on cardboard. Last year, even before I quit swimming, I decided I didn't believe in anything that couldn't be properly explained. I felt comfortable with this. It made things simple. I'm not a little kid anymore and I figured if there wasn't *proof* for something, then it was no more than a fairy tale.

I dislike having a crisis. Trinity should keep them to herself. Now, she's being freakier than ever. She says, "There's no such thing as proof, Safira. You can't even prove that you're here."

I say, "Get real. Of course I can."

"How?" she says.

I reach over and smack her arm. "There you go. You felt that, didn't you?"

"Hmm," she says. "You think I felt it. Maybe even *I* think I felt it. But the fact is, we could be nothing more than brains in a bottle somewhere. Scientists could be poking these brains with little probes. The probes make the brains believe they have bodies and are walking around doing things. Can you prove you're not a brain in a bottle that's part of some sick experiment?"

"I'm not a brain in a bottle."

"Prove it," she says.

I open my mouth. I close it. I think of lots of things to say, like how I have parents who will swear my mom gave birth to me. But what if I've been programmed to believe that? I smell things. I taste things. I feel and hear and see. But if all of that comes out of my brain, then what? I say, "You are so depressing, you know?"

She grins. "Nope. I don't think I'm a brain in a bottle. I think I'm a soul in a body, creating my life. And my soul will go on from here. It's way better to keep proof in its place. Proof is highly overrated."

"How did you get like this?" I ask.

"Like what?"

I don't know exactly what I mean, but say, "You feel so sure about having a soul."

"I've told you before," she says. "When my Mama was pregnant with me, she visited the Philippines and she touched a faith healer, an *Albularyo*. That made some of the healer's traits rub off on me. It helps me be sure."

She *did* tell me this before. I thought it was so dumb. "Okay," I moan. "Let's say you're right. I did see a ghost. And she needs help." I wave my arms around. "I still don't know how to help her."

"Sisters," Trinity murmurs.

"I know. You think her sister killed

her. But what if the Ouija was just messing around with us? What if it heard us talking earlier about being like sisters?"

"Hmm." Trinity's brow wrinkles. "I *guess* that could be it. Or it could be that her sister was murdered too? What we need to find out is if there's a case of death involving sisters."

"How do we do that?"

"Let's start with the washstand," she says. "We'll call the summer camp tomorrow and ask about it. They could pretend to know nothing, so we're going to have to be clever."

"Right," I say. "Clever. Maybe nothing is what it seems. What if we're missing the point of the washstand? What if it's symbolic of, oh, I don't know. Water?"

Trinity stares at me, her brows puckered. "Wow. I never thought of that. Water is so elemental, isn't it? Safira, I think you're going to be really good at this stuff, now that you're allowing yourself to be free."

Enough already. I say, "You know what?

I'm starving. Do you think your mom made *lumpia* today?"

"If she did, she probably took it to my Auntie's house. They were going to have a Karaoke night over there."

I feel a little pang of envy. I would never admit this to anyone other than Trinity, but when they do Karaoke here, I love joining in. It's way more fun than the Ouija. "Ice cream?" I ask hopefully.

"Let's check it out," Trinity says.

And after we've polished off a bowl of chocolate ice cream in the kitchen, I feel much better. I even manage to sleep.

First thing in the morning, Trinity starts nagging me to call the camp. Okay, so it isn't first thing in the morning, because we slept until eleven, but it's the first thing we do. She comes up with a plan for being clever about my questions. And then I'm on the phone with the camp director.

"Hello, this is Safira Nelson calling. I was at camp there last week, remember?

What? No, I didn't lose anything. I'm just wondering about your, um, washstand."

Trinity is hovering beside me, watching like a beady-eyed hummingbird.

"Yes," I say. "That's right. The washstand in the girl's cabin. Can you tell me anything about it?"

Trinity puts her ear to the phone beside mine, and I miss the camp director's reply.

"Pardon? Did you say you don't know anything about it?"

The camp director asks why I want to know about a darn old washstand.

"Careful!" Trinity hisses.

"Well, you see," I say, "I sort of liked that washstand and I was wondering if I might be able to buy it. But I need to know more details, so I can explain it to my parents."

The director laughs.

"No, seriously," I stammer. "It's really cool. Do you know how old it is, or where it came from?"

The director stops laughing long enough to gasp, "You kids these days!"

I feel offended. I mean, why wouldn't

someone want to buy a washstand? It isn't that strange. People are always finding old stuff at yard sales that might seem trashy, but really isn't. "Honest," I say, "I want to explore the history of the washstand."

Right, so maybe that did sound silly. The director goes off in another fit of laughter then finally chokes out, "Thanks for the laugh, dear. Tell you what. If you want that old thing, you just find me a replacement and you can have it." Then she hangs up.

"Hmph!" says Trinity. "She's either very good at hiding what she knows, or she doesn't know a thing."

"My guess is she doesn't know a thing," I say glumly.

"I wonder who owns that camp," Trinity says.

"Oh, no. Uh-uh. Forget it, Trin. I am not going any further with this. Not."

She eyes me. "Fine. I'll take care of the research on that. You focus on staying open to the spirit world. I think that's best. The spirit contacted you, and now that

you're finally starting to see past your nose,
chances are she'll visit you again."

Isn't that a lovely thought? I can't wait.

chapter nine

The days drag on. I've never had such a boring summer and I actually start thinking it would be a good thing to go back to school. That is so not like me. Maybe it's another sign of growing up? Must be a sign of something.

Trinity continues to do research on ghosts, washstands and cases of murder involving sisters. I don't tell her that I now sleep with a night-light on in my room. I don't want any unexpected visitors. When

Trinity's mother finds out what she's up to, she freaks.

"Trinity, you are a crazy girl! Don't you remember when my own Mamang, God rest her soul, died last year?"

Trinity says, "How could I forget?"

"Ah!" says Mrs. Turner. "It was dreadpul. I had to sleep in one room with all six of my sisters por protection. Our Mamang was not so nice, huh? We thought she was going to come back and haunt us, she was so miserable. Por a whole week, we did this. You leave the dead alone!"

"Mama," Trinity says, "Lola didn't come back to haunt anyone. Besides, I'm trying to send Safira's ghost on, not bring her back."

Mrs. Turner frowns. She calls Mr. Turner into the kitchen and tries to get him to convince Trinity. Instead, he laughs and puts his arm around Mrs. Turner. "You are so cute. Did I ever tell you how cute you are?" Then he gives her a great big kiss. Trin and I hustle out of there.

"They are so weird," Trinity mutters.

"Um," I say. "Not really."

"OK, come on, Safira. Look at how *old* they are. Shouldn't they be over that stuff by now?"

She has a point.

As more days trickle past, an awful feeling rumbles in the pit of my stomach and I get the shivers more and more. I've never been the sickly sort, but I start to wonder if there's something seriously wrong with me. Maybe I have a rare form of cancer or some other awful disease? I finally tell Mom about it.

She sighs, pats my arm and says, "We're all feeling nervous, Safira. It's only two more days until the wedding." She looks at me and adds, "Just make sure you get lots of rest and exercise. And don't forget to eat right."

Talk about your standard Mom advice. But since I don't have any better ideas, I follow her advice and go for a run. When I get home, the only one in the house is Mya. As I walk past her room on the way to mine, I notice her door is open. Not normal. Even less normal is the silence. Mya always plays music when she's in her room. I pause at the open door and say, "Hey."

There's the distinct sound of a nose being blown, and a muffled, "What?"

I take a huge risk and step inside. "Are you okay, Mya?"

She's scrunched up on her bed with her back to the door. She says, "Does it look like I'm okay?"

I can't believe she actually said so many words to me. Carefully, I say, "No."

She doesn't answer.

"What's wrong?" I ask.

A huge shuddery sigh comes from the bed. "You wouldn't understand."

"I might," I say. "I could try."

She sits up and squints at me through red puffy eyes. "What the heck. It's this whole deal with Lino and Jill. I mean, I thought we'd worked it out, but Jill's still being strange. And she's been my best friend forever. Like you and Trinity, right?"

I nod.

"But she and Lino hate each other. And it's all so...I don't know. Impossible!"

"I've always liked Jill," I say. "She's nice."

Her dark eyes narrow. Her face pales and her nose turns pink and starts to quiver. Uh-oh. That's the red alert Mom face! The one a smart person avoids. Too late, I realize I should have said I also like Lino. The thing is, I'm too surprised to run. "Do I look like that when I'm mad too?" I ask.

"What?" Mya hisses.

"You look just like Mom right now," I tell her.

Whatever she was going to say is lost. Instead, she leaps from the bed and races to her mirror. "Oh my God!" she wails. "I *do* look like her. My nose...!" She places a finger on her nose and squashes it flat, as if she's trying to squeeze out the pink. It doesn't work. When she removes the finger, her nose is pinker than ever.

"Jill always told me I was like her," she moans. "I thought she was just kidding."

"It's not as if you're exactly like Mom," I say. "I mean, there are plenty of ways you're different."

"Too right." she says. Then her expression gets thoughtful. "What do *you* think of Lino?"

Something must be seriously wrong with her. She's asking me this question, like what I say might actually matter? I feel a huge rush of gratitude that is swiftly washed away in a cold bath of confusion. Do I lie and say Lino's great? I want this sisterly moment to continue. I do. But I can't lie that big. I say, "I don't really know him."

Mya stares at me. She blinks. "Right. Thanks for nothing, Safira."

I blurt, "I mean, I wish I did. Because then I'm sure I'd like him."

She allows herself a small smile. "Oh, yeah, you'd like him. Cuz if you *did* know him, you'd see what a sweetie he is. He cares about me so much and he's always talking about how he's going to look after me."

Now I want to say she's old enough to look after herself, but I don't. I just nod.

Mya goes on. "See, if Jill got to know him better, I'm sure she'd like him too. We just haven't hung out together often enough. Lino always wants me to himself."

"Oh," I say.

She gathers up a section of her hair and studies it. Mya has amazing hair: long, dark, all one even glossy length. Abruptly she says, "I'm going to call Jill right now. I want to get my hair cut for the wedding and I want it to be a surprise for Lino. Maybe Jill will come with me and then we can go for coffee. Like old times."

"Sounds good," I tell her.

And then she turns away, like I just ceased to exist again.

I say, "Catch you later," and slip out of her room. My own room feels safe and, at the same time, boring. I plop onto my bed, stretch out and stare at the ceiling. I should have lied. Then maybe Mya would still be talking to me. Maybe she'd even ask *me* to go with her for the haircut and coffee. I replay the whole scene and get snagged on one thing.

Mya *is* like Mom. She's even getting married at the same age. Not that Lino is anything like Dad. Mom and Dad were both only twenty when they got married; Lino is twenty-six. I picture his face, that chilling blankness he wore when Trinity asked him if he was for real. And I get that shiver again.

Is it true that Mya wants out of our family? Are we really so bad? I don't think so. Okay, Mom and Mya have always fought a lot; it's as if Mya has *always* been fighting to be apart. To be different. Only it seems like there are some things that just can't be wished away, or thought away or even fought away. They're just there, part of who you are. I mean, what do you do about a nose that turns pink when you're mad?

Nothing, I guess.

Obviously, there are some things we *can* change. Mya found plenty. When she graduated from high school, she had big plans to travel and go to university. She got a job and started saving up for a trip to Europe. And then she met Lino and all that changed. Not for the better, so far as I can tell. Does love screw you up like that?

I changed how I felt about swimming. I *did* love it. Dad says it was plain as day when he took me to a toddler class. There was no stopping me. Being in water was like being at home. I swam every chance I got, in pools, lakes, rivers, the ocean. The ocean was the best. It was amazing to be immersed in that huge body of water, to know that it went on, around the earth. It was crazy beautiful, a place of endless possibility.

But last year, it all got twisted. My swim coach pushed me to compete. And practice. And compete. The only place I ever swam was in a pool, and the stop-watch was always ticking. Time became my enemy. At first, I usually won. But when it stopped being fun I started to lose, lose, lose. I hated it! It wasn't just the losing I hated. I could deal with that. It was more like I'd taken the best part of me and made it into a machine. Dad used to laugh so much when we were just goofing around in the water. The competition took his smiles away too. I wonder if he knows that.

Or was it Mya getting engaged to Lino that took Dad's smile away? I never thought of that before. Now that I know he isn't happy about that, I wonder. It all happened around the same time, didn't it?

I'm confusing myself. Maybe I should call Trinity. What was that smart remark she made about the ghost being like swimming? Something about having experiences I can't explain.

No, I can't explain it, but I do remember every detail. It was the final meet. I qualified since I'd done well early in the season. I told Dad and the coach that I didn't want to go, but they both just basically patted my head and said I'd be fine. I wasn't fine.

It happened during the backstroke race. I was doing okay, keeping up with the others, but on the final turn, when I went under, it felt like I'd never come up again. Through the water, I saw my dad waving me on. I glimpsed my coach yelling from the side. There was the stroke-and-turn judge above me, a watery pillar of detached opinion. And then *I* was detached, from myself. I wanted to take a breath. I wanted to go up, not on. I *needed* to break the surface but my push off the wall sent me deep.

I shouldn't have gone so deep. The world exploded into a thousand crazy colors. The colors swirled around me and wrapped around my legs, my chest and my head. As they closed in and squeezed, intense pain ripped through my brain. Then a cloud of black poured over the colors, the cold black of deep shade, and I was dead.

I wasn't dead. They said it was a panic attack, not too common, but not unheard of. It was nothing to worry about. These things happen.

I haven't been in the water since then. I know everyone thinks I'm scared, but that's not it. It's more like...what? Let's scc. Maybe it's like having a dog die and then getting it stuffed and keeping it in the living room? I've heard of people being weird like that. They can't let go of the much-loved dead. If I kept trying to swim, it would be like holding on to something that's dead.

chapter ten

Trinity is on the phone. "Safira, you won't believe it! I think I've found our victim."

"Are you serious?" I ask.

"Yes! For real! Can you come over right now?"

I consider this. "You're not saying you've found, like, an actual body, are you?"

Trinity snorts. "No, goof. Well, maybe. But it's buried."

I feel the need for further clarity. "But we're not going to look at this, um, grave or anything, are we?" With Trinity, one needs to be careful.

"It's possible. Some day. Jeez, Safira, right now I just want to show you a newspaper article, okay?"

I sigh with relief. "Okay. I'll be over in a bit."

When I arrive at Trinity's, she's vibrating with excitement. She waves a piece of paper in my face and says, "Read this."

I take the paper, flop down in a chair and read a copy of an old newspaper article.

LOCAL WOMAN KILLED BY FALL FROM WINDOW.

Miss Myra Norton, 20 years old, was instantly killed late last evening when she fell from a second-story window of her home. It is believed that she may have been attempting to exit through the bathroom window. Scuff marks on the washstand suggest that she used this as a stepping-off point. Dr. Kandt pronounced her dead at the scene.

–Times Colonist, August 20, 1940.

I look up at Trinity. "So? This doesn't mean anything."

She smiles. "Wanna bet? Check this out." And she sets another piece of paper in my lap.

QUESTIONS ARISE IN YOUNG WOMAN'S DEATH

Miss Sarah Norton, sister of the recently deceased, Myra Norton, was detained by police for questioning. A neighbour reported that she overheard the sisters shouting early on the evening of Myra Norton's death. She said the sisters were arguing over the affections of a young man. Police say this person has also been questioned. While it has not been confirmed, it is thought that Myra was attempting to sneak out of the family home for a clandestine meeting with the young man.

—Times Colonist, August 25, 1940.

Further down the page, there is a third blurb about Myra.

FUNERAL SERVICE HELD, QUESTIONS LINGER

Following a small funeral service, Miss Myra Norton was laid to rest today at Mountain View Cemetery. Earlier reports raised questions regarding the circumstances of her death. However, police say the case has now been closed. A neighbour reports that the family has plans to demolish the old family home. They have stated that the old house holds too many painful memories and they wish to build a modern, one-story house.

—Times Colonist, August 29, 1940.

I drop the paper. Trinity, who has been hovering over me, says, "So? What do you think?"

"Where did you find this?" I ask.

She shrugs. "It took a while, but I just kept searching the net until I found it. Then I printed it out. I think Myra is your ghost."

A prickle runs over my scalp. "It does fit, doesn't it?"

"Too right it fits. We've got sisters, death by falling—or being pushed!—off a washstand. I mean, the family probably sold it when the house was demolished, right? And Myra must have stayed with the washstand!"

"Wow. This is creepy. Now what?"

"Now, we need to use the Ouija to get in touch with her. We'll ask if her sister pushed her out the window. Because if that's what happened we'll have to get the police to reopen the case."

I glance down at the date on the article. "Um, Trin? This happened a *long* time ago. Even if her sister did it, and even if she's still alive, she would be ancient by now."

"Yeah," Trinity says, "but if Myra needs justice to be at peace, what else can we do?"

"I don't know," I mutter. "Tell her Elvis is dead now too, and if she moves on she might get to meet him?"

"Safira! That's terrible." She pauses for half a second, and then adds, "It's also dumb. Elvis wasn't big until the nineteen-fifties, before Myra's time. Anyway, how can you joke about this?"

I sigh. "I'm not joking. Think about it. Don't you think she's a few bubbles short of a bath? Would *you* hang out in a washstand for almost seventy years?"

Trinity shrugs. "I doubt it. But possibly she injured her head in the fall and she isn't thinking clearly. Or—she was robbed of her one true love and never got to experience the life she was meant to have. That would really mess up her karma. How can we judge? Oh! I almost forgot! There's a picture of her too, on the net. I couldn't get it to print properly, so you need to check it out on the screen."

I follow her to the computer and wait, with a feeling of dread, while she brings up the picture. But the second I see it...

"That's not her. That is *so* not her."

"What?" Trinity screeches. "Are you sure? It must be her. It's too perfect."

"Sorry," I say. "This is not the same girl. Not a chance. The hair, the chin, the nose—nothing like my ghost."

Trinity gives me a sour look. "You don't have to look so happy about it."

I'm not happy. I'm just super-relieved.

chapter eleven

I'm wakened by a sharp clatter. And just like that time in the cabin, I'm not just sort of awake—I'm *wide* awake. I grab my sheets, draw them up to my chin and then slowly sit up. Carefully, I examine every inch of my room. The night-light provides enough glow for me to see into each corner. I find nothing unusual. I strain to hear, but there's only silence. I take a deep breath in and let it out slowly. Whew. Probably just a racoon knocking over a garbage can. I lie back.

And then I hear a low moan. Every molecule in my body turns to ice with this certain knowledge: *She's here, in my house*! The moan came from the washroom next to my bedroom. Of course she's in the washroom. Where else would she be? I clutch at my sheets and stare at the door. She could decide to come in here, couldn't she? I switch my stare to the wall. She could come right through the wall, couldn't she? Oh, God. Why me? I hear Trinity's voice in my head saying, "You have to help her, Safira."

I ignore Trinity's voice. I can't do this. Not only that, I can't tell Trinity the ghost came back. She'll never forgive me for being a wimp. I'll have to carry this secret with me to my grave. Argh! What a thought. I don't want to think about my grave.

I realize I've been holding my breath, and take in a little gulp of air. What was that? Another sound from the bathroom! I hold my breath again. Oh God, oh God, oh God! Do I believe in God? Yes, I do. I mean, if there's a ghost in the bathroom,

God must exist too, right? What would God do? I have no idea what God would do.

Another sound! A sob. That was a sob; I know a sob when I hear one. Oh, I am such a coward. That poor girl. Enough already. All I have to do is tell her she made a wrong turn somewhere. Happens all the time. People don't get good directions, and bam, they're lost. I can tell her that. I'll tell her to look for the light. That's it. Dead people are supposed to follow the light.

I place one foot on the floor. I place the other foot. I stand. Step. Step. I'm doing it. I'm at my door, I'm opening it. I'm in the hall. There's the bathroom door. There it is. It's half closed. I reach for the knob. Pull back. Reach for the knob. Pull back. Listen. Anything?

Nothing.

I'm probably too late. I dawdled, and now she's drifted out into the street. She's going back to her dingy washstand because I took too long. I failed her.

I reach for the knob and this time, I

take hold of it. I push the door open. The faint light coming from the window is all there is. I take a deep breath. Shall I switch on the light? No. That would scare her away for sure. I inch forward and poke my head around the door frame.

And there she is! The stripes. The dark jagged hair across her forehead. I feel my mouth open wide, feel a scream gathering, and it takes every ounce of willpower I possess to swallow it back down. I don't quite stifle the scream. A gurgle comes out of my throat. She's standing on the toilet, gazing out the window, and when I gurgle, she turns. The hair shadows her eyes. There's that unbearable sadness. It's her all right. It's...

It's...

"Mya?"

"Leave me alone!"

I sag against the door frame. I feel woozy, like maybe I'm going to faint. I stare at my sister and gasp, "Are you dead?"

"Are you nuts?" Mya asks.

"But...," I stammer. "You...She had... Your hair!"

"I got it cut, remember?" she says. And then a giant tear, glistening like a bead of silver, slides down her cheek.

"And you got a new striped top?" I ask.

"Omigod," she moans. She turns back to the window. Her voice crumbles around a sob as she adds, "Please, Safira. Just leave me alone."

In that moment, when she turns her profile to me again, I see something else. "What happened to you? To your face?"

"Nothing! Crap! Would you just go?"

I go. I climb back into my bed and I lie awake for a long time. I think about a lot of things. I think about calling Trinity, but it's the middle of the night. I'm not even sure I'd know what to say. Mostly I think that tomorrow is the day my sister gets married. At some point, I drift into a half sleep and wake from it, startled. I dreamt that I was trying to dive, but my feet were stuck to the ground.

chapter twelve

I wake up early. I peek into Mya's room and once I'm certain that she's really just sleeping, I run to Trinity's house.

Mrs. Turner answers my knock. "Sapira! You are here bright and early. Trinity is still sleeping."

"Do you mind if I go wake her?" I ask.

She grins. "Go ahead. I don't mind one bit. She's the one who may mind, so be carepul."

"I will," I say. But I'm not careful. I jump

on Trinity's bed and start shaking her. "Trin! Wake up! Hurry!"

"Wha...? Oh. Go away." She flaps an arm at me and her eyes remain shut.

"I know who she is, Trin. The ghost. Or whatever. I know."

That gets her attention. Both eyes pop open. "What? You do? How? She came back?"

"She was always there," I say.

Trinity rubs her eyes and sits up. "Huh?"

There's no way to explain it, so I just tell her, "It was Mya."

Trinity collapses back onto her pillow. "You're not making any sense."

"I know. But I'm telling you, I saw Mya in the dark last night. She got her hair cut and she was wearing this striped shirt, and it was exactly her."

"And she looked sad?" Trinity asks.

I nod. "Oh, yeah. Really sad."

Trinity is frowning now. "Have you seen Mya yet today?"

"Yup," she said. "I checked on her. She is in bed sleeping."

"Sleeping?" Trinity squints at me. "Ah. Um. I don't know how to put this, exactly. Safira, are you *sure* Mya wasn't dead?"

"I'm sure."

"And," Trinity says carefully, "did this person speak to you?"

"The person this morning or the person last night?" I ask.

She blinks. "Both, I guess."

"The person last night, Mya, yes. She told me to go away. The person this morning, Mya, no. She snored."

"Whew," Trinity sighs. "That's good. At least for the moment."

"Why is it good?" I ask. I have my own reasons for thinking that, but I want to hear Trinity's too.

"Okay, here's the thing. If the person who visited you at camp was Mya, and if you're sure she didn't actually go there in the flesh to play a trick on you..."

"She didn't have that haircut then," I say.

"Right. And your sister isn't exactly the practical joker type, either, is she? Plus you definitely said the camp visitor was not of this world." Trinity pauses. "I'm afraid that only leaves us with one explanation. The Mya at camp was her shade."

"Her what?"

"It had to be her shade. A shade is something like a ghost, only it's really more like a fetch. Like a shadow of the living person." Trinity takes my hand. "The thing is...a shade sometimes appears to a loved one to say good-bye...just before they're about to die."

"Mya's not going to die," I say.

Trinity looks down. "No," she says softly, "you're probably right."

"She's not!" I say. "I'm not going to let her."

"I believe you," Trinity says.

I can see that she doesn't believe me. She looks sadder than Mya. "Listen, Trin. I did a lot of thinking last night. I didn't know that the thing I saw was called a shade. But I know that if it was my sister, she was asking for help. See, there was another thing too. It looked like Mya had a bruise on her face last night."

"So you think the shade was a warning for the bruise?" Trinity gazes at me with pity.

"No. I think that jerk of a boyfriend, Lino, hit her. I think he didn't like her surprise haircut or her going out with her friend, Jill. I think Mya *will* die if she marries him. I'm not going to let that happen."

Trinity stares at me. "You're serious, aren't you? And you know, I think you could be right. Why couldn't a shade appear to ask for help? That makes sense."

"Too right it makes sense. I think it goes even further than that. I think that when Mya appeared at camp, part of her was dying then. Her spirit. You know how horrible she's been with the wedding—a total Bridezilla? And even though she's always argued with Mom, this past while it's been way worse. And she was upset about losing Jill. And she's lost all her dreams. It's all been killing her!"

"Why didn't she just call it off and break up with Lino, then?" Trinity asks.

"Probably because she couldn't do it on her own. Either she was scared or because her spirit was dying, she was weak."

Trinity shakes her head. "Wow. That's amazing. You're amazing."

"I'm amazing?" I ask.

"Yes. You go deep, Safira. That's what I love about you." Then her eyes widen and she screeches, "The wedding is today!"

"I know," I tell her. "So you're coming with me. I've got it all figured out. When they come to that part in the ceremony—the one when they ask if anyone knows a reason why the couple shouldn't get married..."

Trinity jumps in. "You're going to tell them?"

"Yup. That's exactly what I'm going to do. In front of everyone. So that slimeball Lino can't stop me."

"All right, girlfriend." Trinity says. She gets to her feet and stands tall, all five feet two inches of her. "I'll be there to watch your back."

chapter thirteen

I look closely at Mya before we leave for
the church. There might be a faint mark on
her cheek, but it's mostly hidden under a
smooth layer of makeup. She looks gorgeous
in the elegant gown. I find it interesting
that she hasn't chosen the lace and pink
ribbon dress. I give her a chance to speak
for herself and say, "So, I guess you're not
feeling romantic today, Mya?"

She looks at me with dazed eyes and
says, "I feel fine, thanks."

I want to answer, "Hello? Anybody home?" but before I can, Mom frowns and tells me to get into my aunt's car. "We'll see you at the church, all right?"

When we get to the church I'm ordered to sit in the family row. Luckily, Trinity is able to slip into the row right behind me. Then we sit there, waiting, for what feels like hours. I start to have doubts. I was so certain that I had it all figured out last night. I was still certain when I explained it to Trinity. But sitting here in the church, with a hundred people all decked out in fancy clothes, I'm not so sure. What if I'm wrong?

I'm wrong. Trinity and all her wacky ideas have made me crazy. Do I really intend to stop a wedding that cost my parents a fortune? Do I really have the courage to stand up in front of all these people and tell them my sister sent her shade so I could save her? They'll probably send an ambulance to save me.

And then Lino slides in. He and his groomsmen emerge from a side door at the front like snakes slithering out from under a rock. Yuck. He's wearing black and his sneer. His sunglasses dangle from his jacket pocket. He takes up his position and stands there like he owns the place. I catch him glancing sideways at one of his pals and rolling his eyes. Oh, yeah, I'm taking that puppy down. I'm right.

The music starts. The minister takes his place. And here come the bridesmaids, wafting up the center aisle like flowers on a breeze. They are so pretty. Okay, Jill doesn't look her best; she's not even smiling. And finally, there's Mya, eyes glazed, smile frozen. Dad walks beside her, holding her arm. There's this strange moment when it looks like he's pulling her along. Like she's a little girl who doesn't want to go. I'm right.

The ceremony starts. I glance back at Trinity, and her eyes are enormous. She looks poised for flight as she gives me a fluttery thumbs-up. Right. I can do this. I listen carefully. There are prayers. The minister speaks about love and the meaning of marriage. I wait. Any minute now, he's going to ask that question. My body feels like a thread pulled tight, to the breaking point.

But wait a minute. He's starting the vows. He's got Mya and Lino facing each other. He's saying, "Repeat after me. Do you, Lino..."

"Wait!" I scream. "Stop! You didn't ask if anyone knows a reason why they shouldn't get married. I know a reason."

I don't know how I got here, but I'm standing in front of the minister, right beside my sister. She's staring at me, her face pale with shock—so pale under that makeup that I can see the bruise clearly.

"Look!" I point at her cheek. "He hit her."

"Good heavens...," the minister sputters.

All around me, I hear the rise of voices, the gasps and murmurs, and my mother saying, "Safira! What...?"

I'm aware of Trinity at my side, her hand clasping my arm. There's a blur of black, Lino reaching out, and I shout, "If she marries him, he's going to kill her!"

The black blur connects with my shoulder. I'm shoved hard, sent staggering backward. "You little snot!" Lino roars.

I don't fall. Trinity holds me up. And then my sister's bouquet, her beautiful bouquet of roses is squashed into Lino's chest. Mya holds it there like a shield and screams, "Don't you dare touch my sister!"

She glares at him, face pale, nose pink and quivering. "You! Look at you. What was I thinking?"

"Babe," he says. But it isn't said sweetly. It sounds like a warning.

Mya snorts. "I'm not your babe. You pushed my little *sister*? That's sick."

He raises his hand again, but it goes nowhere. My dad is there, one of the groomsmen too, and Jill pulls Mya out of range. To Lino, Dad says, very softly, "You better go now." For half a second, Lino looks like he's going to argue. But the groomsman tugs on his arm, and Lino leaves. Every eye in the church follows him out the door.

Mom is with us now too, clasping my hand, clasping Mya's. Her voice trembles as she asks, "Did he really hit you?"

In a clear voice she says, "No." She touches the bruise on her cheek. "This is just a giant zit I tried to get rid of and it sort of..." She stops, glances at the watching crowd and gives an embarrassed little shrug. Then she looks at me. "But Safira was right. If I'd married him, I would have died."

chapter fourteen

Trinity and I are in my room, replaying every detail of the events at the church. Trinity tells me my nose was bright pink. I'm trying to decide if this makes me happy or not, when Mya and Jill walk in. Wow. They've never visited my room before.

Mya says, "So, Sis. I need to know. How did *you* know?"

"It's like this," I say. I start at the beginning, telling them about Mya's appearance at camp. They're completely stunned, hanging on my every word. It's great.

Trinity jumps in. "Can I tell the next part? Please?"

I nod and Trinity picks up the story. That girl is destined for a career on the stage or maybe in politics. Her performance is incredible. She makes me proud. Mya and Jill are amazed at the amount of research Trinity did. They're speechless over the message of the Ouija. They puzzle over Myra Norton.

"Her name was *Myra*?" Mya asks. "That's freaky."

"Yeah," Jill agrees. "Just take one letter out of the name and you've got Mya. Makes you wonder."

"True," Trinity says, "but it's also a heads up for me. In the realm of the paranormal, coincidence can lead us astray."

I grin at her. "Like auras in pictures? You're saying we can read too much into some things?"

She giggles, then grows serious again. "So maybe there wasn't an aura around the washstand. But there *was* a real mystery. And someone did need your help, right? The main thing is, you figured it out, Safira."

She's right. But at the moment, there's something else I need to figure out. "Mya? What happened to you? With Lino, I mean."

She gazes out the window and shakes her head. "I don't know. I think it's going to take a while to understand. It hurts."

I press on. "Did you love him?"

She nods. "I think I did. But then... it wasn't *right*. At first, he seemed so mysterious. He was such a cool guy, and I was so flattered that he was interested in me. He seemed more exciting than anything I had going on, ever. And then he started to take over, you know? He thought university was a waste of time. He thought Europe was just a bunch of boring old buildings. He wanted me with him, every minute."

She pauses and shakes her head again. "He even had me convinced that my family and friends were a bunch of control freaks. I think that was the weirdest part about it.

Every time I told him about something that didn't fit in with the Lino way, he mocked it. He twisted things. I'd feel like what he was saying was wrong, yet I couldn't find the flaw. Like when I got my haircut. He was furious that I hadn't asked him. He said he loved my hair just the way it was and how could I go behind his back like that? Didn't I care how he felt?"

"It's *your* hair," I say.

"I know. He was even angrier that I'd gone with Jill. He said she's the sneaky one. She must have talked me into it because she wants to be in charge of me."

"What?" Jill screeches. "*He* was the control freak."

"Yeah," Mya says softly. "He was. And somewhere along the way, I lost myself. I guess that sounds stupid, but it's as if I was living in his shadow. I didn't know who I was anymore."

"Except Bridezilla?" Trinity asks.

Mya bursts out laughing. "That bad, eh?"

There are nods all around.

"But I still don't get it," I say. "You always seemed strong, Mya. Confident. How could this happen to you?"

She shrugs. "Like I said, I still don't know. It wasn't sudden—it was gradual. And obviously I wasn't as strong as I pretended to be. Mom was right. I wasn't ready. She and Dad tried to talk me out of getting married. Did you know that? But I threw it in their faces, how they'd gotten married young. And of course Lino made sure I saw them as controlling."

I get that shiver. "I hope that never happens to me," I mutter.

Mya looks at me. "Safira, if you're ever in trouble, promise me something."

"What?"

"Promise you'll send me your shade, okay? I'll be there in a heartbeat."

"You'll be scared," I tell her.

"Of you?" she scoffs. "I don't think so."

chapter fifteen

A week rolls by, enough time for me to start feeling restless again. It's not exactly boredom. I've been doing a lot of thinking when I'm not listening to Mom and Mya argue. That doesn't happen too often anymore, but they're at it again today.

Mom says, "We don't expect you to pay us back, Mya."

"But I have to," Mya says. "I know it means you'll have to put up with me living at home for a couple more years—"

"Put up with you?" Mom interrupts. "Mya, it's not like that. We just want you to get on with your life, follow those dreams you have."

"First, I need to pay you back," Mya says.

Mom sighs. "We'll work something out. I just hope you can be happy. Be all you can be."

Be happy. Be all you can be. Those words ring and echo and bug me, big time. I'm not really happy. I'm not really unhappy. I have no idea what I can be. I only know something I *can't* be. I do feel good about saving Mya from Lino, but it's not like that's going to happen again. At least, I hope not.

The problem is that I still don't understand some things. And no matter how hard I try to figure out how a shade is possible or how a panic attack can happen, I can't. I'd really like it if things went back to normal. Whatever that is.

I call Trinity and ask her, "What is normal?"

She says, "I'll be right over. We can decide when I get there."

I wait for her in the backyard. It's a warm day, the sun shining in a wide-open blue sky. I lie down on the grass and gaze upward, trying to decide if *I'm* normal. I'm thinking so hard that I don't notice Mya until she speaks.

"Must be a big question," she says.

"What?"

She laughs. "You look like you're trying to figure out quantum physics."

I frown at her. "Huh?"

"Never mind. You'll get to that later." She studies me for a minute. "For now, just enjoy being a kid, okay?"

"Um. Yeah." I return my gaze to the sky. "Now all I need to know is how to do that."

"You used to love swimming," she says.

"Right," I mutter. "I *used* to."

"So," she says, "maybe you just need to try something else."

"Like what?"

She shrugs. "That's for you to figure

out. And you will. I need to do the same thing."

This surprises me. "You don't know what you want to do?"

"Nope." She sighs. "I'm not the same person I was. I guess that's life, eh? The only thing you can count on staying the same is that everything changes."

I wrinkle my nose. "That stinks."

"Not really." She smiles. "Look at how great it is that we can talk like this now."

I smile back. "Yeah. That is pretty great."

We sit in silence for a few minutes. Then I blurt, "I just didn't like competing. I still love the water." What is it with this stuff that comes out of nowhere?

She raises an eyebrow. "Yeah? So what are you going to do about it?"

"I don't know. I feel like I let Dad down."

"I know what that's like," she says. "But if you tell him the truth you might be surprised at how cool he can be."

Before I can answer, Trinity flies into the backyard. "Hey, Safira. Hey, Mya. So I figured it out."

Mya and I look at her. In unison, we ask, "What?"

Trinity grins. "There's no such thing as normal."

"Okay," Mya says. "I'll go along with that."

I groan. "No normal. Everything changes."

"For sure," Trinity says. "So, what do you want to do?"

I look at her. I look at Mya. I say, "Let's go for a walk. To the beach."

"All right!" Trinity leans down and grabs my hand. "On your feet, girl, before you change your mind."

I let her pull me up and turn to Mya. She shakes her head. "You two go ahead. I'll catch you later."

We set out walking, but after a few minutes, Trinity says, "Uh, Safira? Can you slow down just a bit?"

"What do you mean?" I ask.

She gives me an eye roll. "You're practically running. What's the rush?"

I glare at her. "I'm not running."

"If you say so," she says.

I mimic the movie version of running in slow motion. "Is this better?"

"Fine with me." She gives me a sideways look. "So. Things seem good with you and Mya."

"Yeah. It's nice." I return the sideways look. "And I figured out something about the shade."

"You did? What?"

"It's sort of hard to put into words," I say. "But I think people in the same family have a special connection. It's like we're tied to each other."

"For sure. My family is like that." Her brow wrinkles. "Do you think it's just being in the same gene pool that makes the connection?"

"No," I say slowly. "I think it's how much we care. I bet if you sent me a shade, I'd notice."

"That's good to know. Thanks!"

"Hey, anytime." I turn to look at her. "But there's something else I figured out. You know how I stopped believing in anything mystical? I thought it was kid stuff? Mya's shade didn't just save her—it saved that part of me too. I believe again. In possibility. And you helped me see that."

Trinity shrieks with delight, "That's awesome, Safira!"

I giggle. "Yeah. *Awe*-some!" With a jolt, I realize my feet have landed on sand. The beach. I look up and feast my eyes on the ocean. "And there's something else. Do you think we can send ourselves a shade?"

Trinity ponders. "Maybe. I mean, we can't really understand how shades work, anyway, can we?"

I keep my gaze fixed on the water. "No. We can't. But we don't need to understand *everything*, do we?"

"Nope," Trinity says. "That would be boring."

The water looks cool, blue. Inviting. There's the sun and sky, the whole world here above. And then there's that watery, shadowy place below: the mysterious world beneath the surface.

Softly, I say, "It really would be boring."

Trinity grins.

"So, why not let some things go?" I kick off my shoes and curl my toes into the soft sand. "And just go for some things?"

As I wade into the water and gather myself for a dive, I'm so happy I start laughing. That's not good because when I dive in, salt water goes up my nose and down my throat. I come up spluttering.

Right. I *do* know a few things about water: There might be undercurrents. Keep trusted companions nearby. Never take it for granted. Always allow for wonder.

I dive again.

Once, long ago, K.L. Denman saw a ghost that was very much like the apparition who appears in this story. Although K.L. never learned the identity of her visitor or the meaning of that strange incident, writing *The Shade* provided her with an enjoyable dip back into the inexplicable. While she hopes never to meet a ghost again, she's delighted that they and many other mysteries exist. She lives and writes in Powell River, British Columbia.